# Comes Joy in the Morning

### Coloring Through Infant Loss & Miscarriage

Compiled by
Lauren Bourne

Burkhart Books

PULON PRESS

Scripture quotations marked NKJV are taken from the New King James Version®. Copyright © 1982 by Thomas Nelson. Used by permission. All rights reserved.

Scripture quotations marked NIV are taken from the THE HOLY BIBLE, NEW INTERNATIONAL VERSION®, NIV® Copyright © 1973, 1978, 1984, 2011 by Biblica, Inc.® Used by permission. All rights reserved worldwide.

Scripture quotations marked MSG are taken from THE MESSAGE, copyright © 1993, 1994, 1995, 1996, 2000, 2001, 2002 by Eugene H. Peterson. Used by permission of NavPress. All rights reserved. Represented by Tyndale House Publishers, Inc.

Cover design by Jason Ratner

Published by

Bedford , Texas

in association with

PULON
PRESS

**THE ARTIST IS IDENTIFIED ON THE PAGE FOLLOWING THE ARTWORK.**

# Bethany Lee

Cheraw, South Carolina
www.pitterandglink.com

Through the suffocating darkness of my many years of infertility and two miscarriages, one fact that has brought me comfort is that God promises us,

*"Weeping may endure for a night, but joy comes in the morning."*

Psalm 30:5 NKJV

Although I still remain childless, I can truly say that I see the sun peeking over the horizon. The darkness is fading, and I am experiencing joy—the kind of joy that only God can give. It's a joy that comes from being aware of my many blessings and having faith that God will fulfill His promises to me.

# Brittany Baker

Denver, CO
www.littlemountainmomma.com

*"Because of the Lord's great love we are not consumed,
for his compassions never fail.
They are new every morning;
great is your faithfulness."*

Lamentations 3:22-23 NIV

The morning sunrise is a constant that has sustained me through the most difficult seasons of life. During a battle with postpartum depression; in the days after the loss of our babies and now as we continue to pray for another baby. The rising sun serves as a daily reminder, that while the world spins madly on around me, God is still on the throne. His love for me is audacious. His compassion for me is unwavering.

# Dreama Camphuysen

Montpelier, VA
www.facebook.com/InkDoodlebyDreama

Though I have not personally experienced miscarriage or infancy loss, many of my dearest friends have had to endure it. My journey to motherhood had its own trials with seven years of trying to conceive. Four of those years were unexplained and we later learned that we had a male factor issue and a one percent chance at a natural conception. After two failed IUI's we moved to IVF and finally welcomed our sweet fraternal twin boys in September 2012 after our third IVF transfer. The scripture in this coloring page is what helped to guide me through all of those years of trying without knowing, having such a slim chance once we finally realized the cause of our infertility, and during all of the failed procedures ...."but as for me, I will always have hope" and I hope with this, you will continue to as well.

# Carrie Fisher

Kennesaw, GA
www.itsybitsystore.etsy.com
www.itstheeveryday.com

When I created this piece I was going through my second miscarriage. Scripture and prayer were surrounding me in my journey of grief. I am so thankful for His Word because of all the promises He gives us. This verse, Psalm 42:8 was a beautiful reminder to me. I added in birds specifically for this one because of the reference to singing in the verse. The birds are always singing to their Creator, and even in the night some have a song to sing. I wanted this to be true of my own heart. Even in the darkness of grief and loss, I wanted to ask the Lord to bring a song to my heart that I can sing back in praise to Him. He is beautiful and will bring that song, and His light into those dark places. Just wait for Him. I am learning this and as I write about this piece I can see places He has given me a song from our own walk in miscarriage.

# Billy Bourne

Fort Worth, TX
www.iamfruitful.org

One of the hardest things for me during our miscarriages was having everyday conversations with people when they expected to see my normal personality. I didn't feel like it. In fact, I felt like I was rotting from the inside out, and people could tell.

Joy, Hope, Peace, and Love were the 4 choices I tried to make. As they slowly crept back in, I could feel the change, and the fruit followed. No matter how small, I was convinced to take small steps in those directions. I Am Fruitful.

BLESSED is She who BELIEVED THAT THE LORD would Fulfill HIS PROMISES to → HER

# Lauren Bourne

Fort Worth, TX
www.iamfruitful.org

God had told us multiple ways that we would have children, and yet we lost three babies while we were trying to grow our family. When our circumstances didn't line up with what God said, we continued to believe. Of course, He is faithful! Two gorgeous children later, we understand what it means to have hope in the middle of hard, to believe even when it looks impossible. If God has given you a promise, cling to it!

# Melissa Aulds

Roanoke, TX
www.melissaaulds.com

*"I'm so sorry, there is no heartbeat."*

In April of 2010 we were devastated when our 12 week appointment showed that I had a Missed Miscarriage. Our little Jasmine had quietly slipped away weeks before. The storm in our lives continued to rage when, in August, we lost another sweet baby girl, our Lily. It was the most painful season of my life, but through it all He held our hearts. Our story blossomed to one of great joy. Our daughter Victoria was born in June of 2011 and our family on earth was completed when Benjamin was born in June of 2012.

# Katie Miller

Decatur, AL
www.anartistinthehomestead84.wordpress.com

One of my favorite quotes is:

*"Where God closes a door, somewhere he opens a window."*

I never thought God would close the door on us concerning children. But maybe, just maybe God will open a window for us, another avenue for the children we've always dreamed of! That is my daily prayer.

# Lauren Bourne

Fort Worth, TX
www.iamfruitful.org

Losing a baby is indescribably hard. It can feel as though you have no strength left and can bring intense fear about your future. I want to encourage you to wake up every morning and clothe yourself with God's strength. Allow Him to show you what joy looks like. Allow Him to cover your fear in His perfect love. Trade in your concerns and receive His peace.

God is a redeeming Father, and when we experience loss, we are positioned to receive double what was stolen! It's a punch in the devil's face when we can hold our head high and laugh while we say, "Devil, you stole something from me, but I rebuke you and I'm now positioned to receive double what I lost!" If it's not in quantity, it will be in quality because God is true to His word!

# Lindsey Hornkohl

Oceanside, CA

http://elindseyhornkohlart.blogspot.com

The whole chapter of Psalm 91 is such a beautiful reminder that we can go to the Lord when we feel broken. He truly is a resting place and a refuge of safety when we're in trouble. God shelters us, rescues us, and protects us. When fear is crippling, we can turn to Him, and He promises to be with us in times of trouble.

# Nikki Boles

Keller, TX

Our family lost two babies through back to back miscarriages after having our two sons. We got pregnant not long after the second miscarriage and now have a beautiful daughter. God is faithful and we want to encourage any families going through a loss or miscarriage that you're not alone. God will restore all that was lost and bring victory to your situation. This page represents a way to remember our babies we lost. Although we can't hold them in our arms we can always remember them and hold them in our hearts. The empty space is for you to write the name of the baby or babies you have lost. We will always remember our Nora and Wyatt.

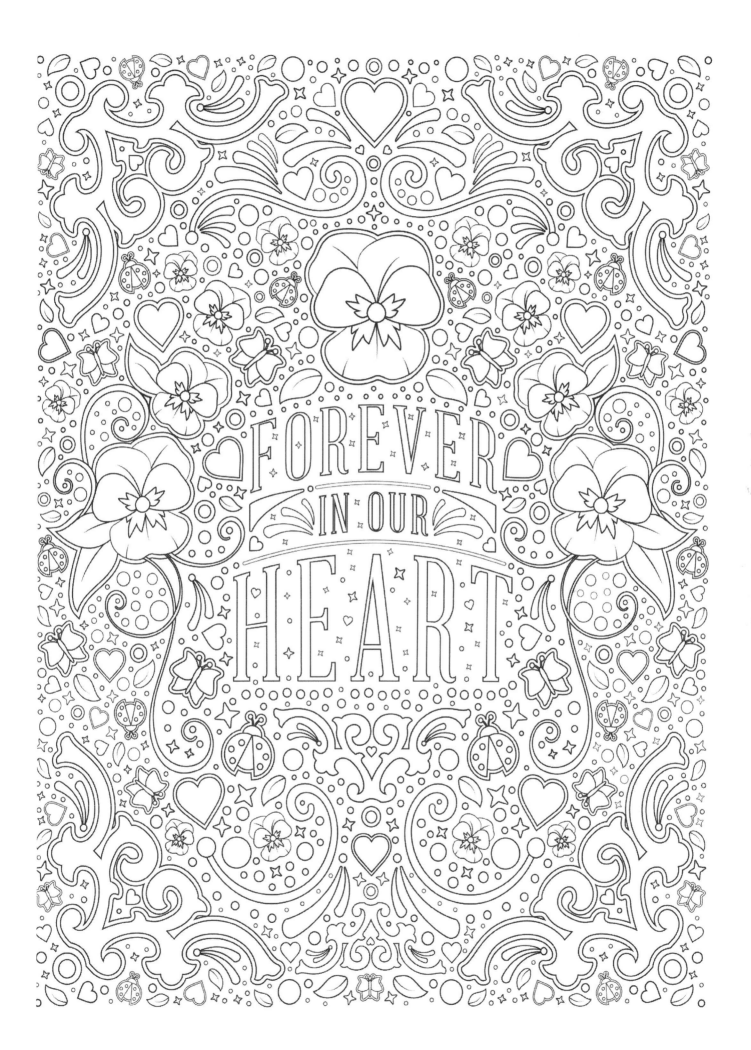

# Jason Ratner

Winter Garden, FL
www.jratnerdesign.com

On February 24, 2015 we gave birth to a beautiful baby girl named Violet, but sadly she was stillborn at 37 weeks. Nothing could really prepare us for something like this and then figure out how to live through the days ahead. With the tremendous support of so many loving friends and family, we have been finding our ways to grow stronger each and everyday. My design is based on the special elements that remind us that she is forever in our heart. Many people believe that their angel sends them signs that they are with them. We think of Violet every time we see a ladybug, butterfly and of course violet flowers. I hope in some way this helps others to think of their angels and keep their memory alive.

# Ashley Haake

Fairmont, MN
www.magnoliamagenta.com

My hope, my prayer is to encourage you in the midst of pain and darkness to focus on Jesus. Set your mind on things above. Look into His eyes of love and know that you can trust His heart and His love for you.  God alone is our hope. I love Psalm 62:6-8 (NKJV):

*"He only is my rock and my salvation, my stronghold; I shall not be shaken.*
*On God my salvation and glory rest; The rock of my strength, my refuge is in God.*
*Trust in Him at all times, O people; Pour out your heart before Him;*
*God is a refuge for us."*

# Brittany Baker

Denver, CO
www.littlemountainmomma.com

*"I have loved you with an everlasting love …."*

Jeremiah 31:3 (NIV)

For three full evenings after the loss of our first baby, the Colorado sky was colored with threads of pink and orange weaved through the iridescent clouds over the Rocky Mountains. In the midst of some of the most intense grief I had ever felt, it was as if God was painting the sky to remind me of the greatness of His love. As I drew this picture I imagined a little mountain town filled with families in need of a reminder of God's powerful and everlasting love.

# Elisa Carrasco

Pilot Point, TX
www.believedespite.org

We are 15 year veterans of infertility with 9 miscarriages and 1 infant death. When our only Earth-born daughter, Crea Jacqueline, passed away, she taught us to Believe Despite. Things were not the way we wanted them to be but felt His gentle whisper, "My ways are not your ways and my thoughts are not your thoughts." Our daughter had cleft lip and palette and my brother drew this cartoon after she passed at my request. It is an honor to share her with you in hopes that as you color these pages, you too will be inspired to Believe Despite and know He is Faithful to complete what He has begun in you.  I say to myself, "

*The Lord is my portion;  therefore I will wait for him."*
*Lamentations 3:24 (NIV)*

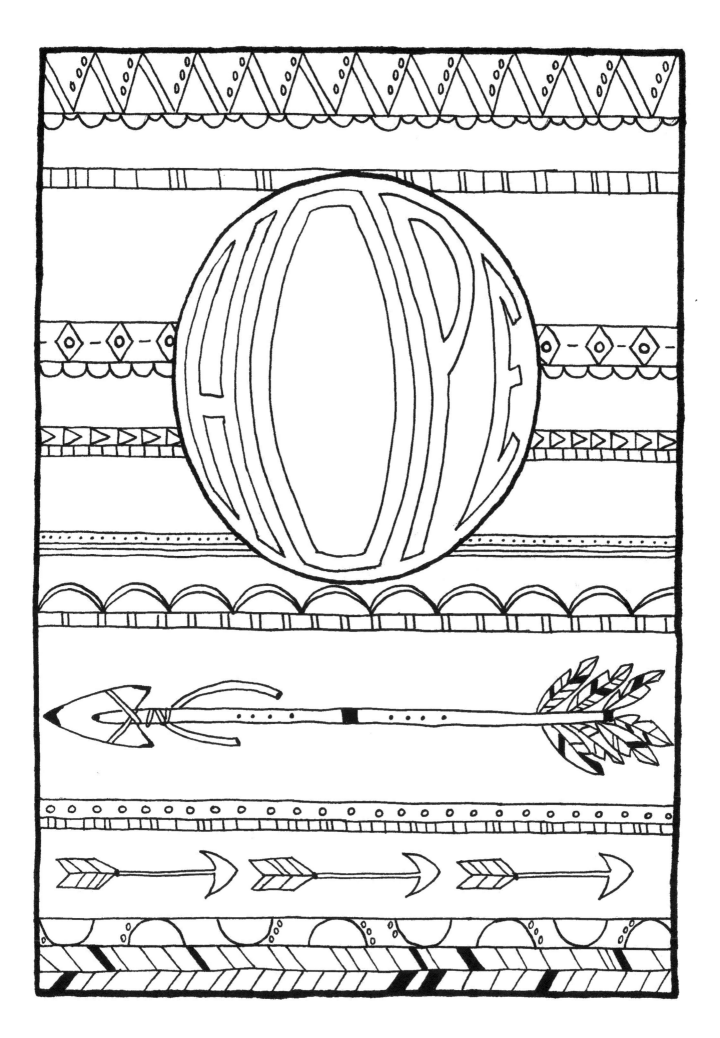

# Lauren Bourne

Fort Worth, TX
www.iamfruitful.org

Always hope. And I'm not talking about simply hoping things get better. I'm talking about joyfully anticipating the good things God has for you regardless of what your situation says. He is good, He is faithful, and He has good things planned for you. Jeremiah 29:11 (MSG) says:

> *"… I know what I'm doing. I have it all planned out, plans to take care of you, not abandon you, plans to give you the future you hope for."*

You will get through this. It will get better. Continue to put your hope in Christ as you grieve this loss of life. He is a redeeming Father, and I pray He restores double what was lost!

Let us not become weary in doing good.

For at the proper time

we will reap a harvest if we do not give up.

Galatians 6:9 (NIV)

# Sheena Demello

Ewa Beach, HI

Aloha! My name is Sheena and Lamentations 3:19-36 helped me see the light during a dark time of loss. I wrote the scripture down in the form of a letter from God to myself and husband. The scripture literally came to life! Each night I would read this letter to myself and it filled me with the momentum of hope. After 10 long years of infertility, endometriosis, surgery, countless IUI's, two failed IVF attempts a miracle happened: we conceived naturally! But our joy soon became bitter sweet when we had a miscarriage at 9 weeks. I decided to share this scripture with you because even through loss, I am still a believer in God's promises. My hope is that you can find peace and comfort in God's word as you and I wait for those promises to be fulfilled.

# Lindsey Hornkohl

Oceanside, CA

http://elindseyhornkohlart.blogspot.com

Joel 2:25 says:

*"I will give back what the locusts have eaten."*

This is the verse I clung to as a promise during my own infertility. The interesting thing is that He doesn't repay in currency that we always expect; God's economy is different than the world's.

# Jennifer Blossom

Anchorage, AK
www.blossomtobefit.com

Jennifer here and I'm so thankful to be able to provide you with a little love and inspiration throughout your fertility journey. I pray that you are inspired, uplifted, and rest assured in God's perfect timing for your life. Although we don't always know the answer, the reason, or the timing, we have to understand that HE is faithful and HE has a perfect plan for your story. So embrace it, girl. Live your life with grace, love, and light. You are blessed and HE will bless you. Have faith and pray bold. He hears it.

# Lauren Bourne

Fort Worth, TX
www.iamfruitful.org

Psalm 30:5 (NIV) is truly the foundation for this coloring book:

*"Weeping may last through the night, but joy comes in the morning."*

One version says, "a shout of joy comes in the morning." What a great reminder when we experience such a deep loss. This is hard. It's so hard. But because we serve a good and redeeming God—you will be able to give a shout of joy in the morning! As you color these pages and continue processing your grief, we pray that God fills you with true hope and that you can begin joyfully anticipating what He has in store for you.

# Lex Ward

Carlsbad, CA
www.thevisualrepublic.com

"You make all things new." What a word to hold onto, especially when you're in the middle of loss or waiting. After 4 years of waiting and hoping to conceive I felt stuck and overlooked. I felt like my "unexplained" diagnosis meant that something huge was wrong and no one could see it. Thank goodness for God's word. Whenever I feel stuck, overlooked or alone I can find such hope in God's word, hope that He is giving me a new beginning today.

# Katie Miller

Decatur, AL
www.anartistinthehomestead84.wordpress.com

I'm thankful for the memory and the legacy your sweet short lives have left us. I learned to love more deeply, to cherish each moment. To care, to cry, to let go, to let God, to carry my burdens to Him, what it truly means to have joy, to have true peace, to share, even when it hurts the most. I love you both so much! I can't begin to thank the Lord for you boys and the lessons I've learned in giving birth to you two!

# Leigh Thompson

Deland, FL

After losing our son Asher at almost 20 weeks pregnant. The Lord was taking me on a journey. Drawing came during a part of the journey where I was starting to actually heal. Everyday I would wake up and spend time with Jesus, and on one of those healing days, this picture and these words are what flowed out of my time with Him. Today, as I write this. God in His perfect wisdom and timing brought our rainbow in my womb. Keep trusting, leaning on Jesus. Your time is coming!! Our God is a God of miracles. Never give up.

# Elizabeth Sanders

Greenville, SC
www.emersonirisphotography.com

Light in the dark, hope in our despair, and strength when we can't keep going on our own; thankful we serve a God that is all those things to us plus more and will never leave our side. After the loss of our daughter at birth, I came across this verse after seeing three beautiful double rainbows within 4 days. The Lord certainly took us under his wing and provided comfort, peace, strength, and hope, and I shout for joy knowing He is always there, always good, and His plans are perfect.

# Carrie Fisher

Kennesaw, GA
www.itsybitsystore.etsy.com
www.itstheeveryday.com

When I created this piece I was actually in the middle of our second miscarriage. It was a really hard time in my life, but having gone through miscarriage once, I knew a little more of what to expect. God's faithfulness was the prevailing theme I took away from my last loss, and not surprisingly He continued to show Himself faithful and as my Sustainer in this miscarriage. In my reading and quiet times with the Lord He gave me this promise in Ephesians 3:20. Hand lettering and drawing scripture is a way that has helped me heal in this process of grief. I knew that this verse needed to be one I could share with others that were walking the same road. It has encouraged my heart and continues to remind me that He really is able to do more (abundantly!) than we can ever imagine!

# Lindsey Hornkohl

Oceanside, CA

http://elindseyhornkohlart.blogspot.com

What a good Father we have that He encourages us to take any and every situation to Him in prayer. The Message (MSG) Version of Philippians 4:6-7 puts it this way:

*"Don't fret or worry. Instead of worrying, pray. Let petitions and praises shape your worries into prayers, letting God know your concerns. Before you know it, a sense of God's wholeness, everything coming together for good, will come and settle you down. It's wonderful what happens when Christ displaces worry at the center of your life."*

You can take the good, the bad, and the ugly to the Lord. He cares about every area of your life!

*I Am Fruitful* is a public charity in DFW, Texas and was founded by Billy and Lauren Bourne to inspire hope in those dealing with delayed fertility and suffering through infant loss and miscarriage. Because of what God did through their own season of miscarriage and waiting, the founders have a deep desire to support couples by teaching on identity, purpose, and the goodness of God.

Through unique programs and resources, *I Am Fruitful* is committed to coming alongside you to encourage and help you experience Christ in a more personal and fulfilling way during your season of waiting. They mentor couples in their home, host free live-streaming videos, and continue to expand their programs and resources—all to help re-ignite your passion for God, stir your hope, and remind you who you are in Christ.

To get connected and download their free devotional, go to:

# www.iamfruitful.org

Made in the USA
Columbia, SC
17 September 2021

45679412R00033